The Sister Book

a guide to good times with your family

by Kristi Thom

illustrated by Brenna Vaughan

★ American Girl®

Published by American Girl Publishing
Copyright © 2015 American Girl

Questions or comments? Call 1-800-845-0005, visit **americangirl.com,** or write to
Customer Service, American Girl, 8400 Fairway Place, Middleton, WI 53562-0497.

Printed in China
15 16 17 18 19 20 21 LEO 10 9 8 7 6 5 4 3 2 1

Editorial Development: Darcie Johnston
Art Direction and Design: Jessica Meihack
Production: Jeannette Bailey, Jill Koshollek, Judith Lary, Paula Moon, Kristi Tabrizi
Illustrations: Brenna Vaughan
Special thanks to Jane Annunziata, PsyD

Library of Congress Cataloging-in-Publication Data

Thom, Kristi
The sister book : a guide to good times with your family / by Kristi Thom ; illustrated by Brenna Vaughan.
pages   cm
ISBN 978-1-60958-977-6 (pbk.) — ISBN 978-1-60958-975-2 (ebook)
1. Sisters—Juvenile literature. 2. Brothers and sisters—Juvenile literature. 3. Families—Juvenile literature.
I. Vaughan, Brenna, illustrator. II. Title.
HQ759.96.J33 2015   306.85—dc23   2014038859

Dear Reader,

Who's always home for a party? Who's with you on family vacations? Who's with you when your friends are not? Your brothers and sisters, that's who!

In these pages, you'll find all kinds of ideas for celebrations and activities to do together. And more than that, *The Sister Book* offers solid advice on how to get through rough stuff with siblings, how to support them through hard times as well as happy ones, and how to share your space. To inspire you, there's even advice from real girls and stories from real sisters.

Your siblings are your built-in buddies, sharing the good and the not-so-good. *The Sister Book* will help you make the most of that special bond—and help you make memories that will keep you smiling years from now.

So why wait? Jump in and get started!

Your friends at American Girl

Contents

p. 73

p. 63

 SAFETY NOTES

Any time you see this hand or when you think a project or recipe is too hard to do yourself, ask an adult to help you. Be sure an adult supervises any cutting or cooking. Also make sure you keep small pieces, such as beads and rhinestones, put away so that younger siblings don't eat them!

The ideas in this book are for girls age 8 and older. If you'd like to do an activity with a younger sibling, always check with an adult first.

p. 80

Real Sister Story

GABRIELLE & HAYLEY

IDENTICAL TWINS Gabrielle and Hayley are not *exactly* alike. Even though they were born eight minutes apart, their birthdays are on different days—November 10 and November 11!

Still, these 12-year-olds have a lot in common. "We're good friends," says Gabrielle (who goes by the nickname Gabri), "and we're both into sports"—including cross country, track, and basketball. Gabri and Hayley also like to draw, and they play on the same volleyball team, but Gabri says she's better at setting and Hayley is better at overhand serving.

Sports aren't the only thing these sisters have in common. "We have a book club," says Hayley, and Gabri adds, "We like the same kind of books." Also, says Hayley, "We're both funny, and we both like making things."

They're in sixth grade at the same school, have the same teacher, and even share the same friends. In fact, the sisters have so much in common that it's almost easier to list the ways they are *not* alike. "I like to watch birds, but Gabri would rather do something else," says Hayley. "And I like popcorn," says Gabri, "but she hates it."

When it comes to being twins, "sometimes people think it would be really annoying to be together all the time," says Gabri. Not true, says Hayley. When people get them mixed up, it doesn't bother them most of the time. "We have switched places on purpose," says Hayley. "We went into the bathroom, switched clothes, then started acting like each other. It worked, and we thought it was so funny that we had to give ourselves away." To help remind people which twin is which, Gabri likes to wear green because green starts with the letter G—just like her name.

Gabri and Hayley have three more siblings, but usually the two of them get along with each other best of all. For Hayley, having a twin means there's always someone around for doing art or practicing a sport. Gabri says, "It's really fun." And—no surprise—Hayley feels the same way. ♥

GO TEAM

SCORE

I LOVE
SPORTS

Everyday Magic

You and your siblings don't have to wait for holidays and other special occasions to come around. Magical memories can be made any day of the year!

Magical Memories

Many families have special things they do again and again to celebrate meaningful days and events.

Maybe your dad makes a special breakfast for you and your brother on the first day of school every fall. Maybe your family leaves "Boo!" gifts for your neighbors at Halloween. Maybe you get a new book every year for Christmas or Hanukkah. These special things are called *traditions*. Traditions come in all kinds of shapes and sizes, and they're different for every family. What traditions does your family have?

Traditions don't have to be a big deal to be very special—almost magical—to your family. You don't have to make something or buy something or spend lots of time getting it ready. What matters is that it means something to all of you.

Because your traditions are so special to you, you'll probably think about them for years and years. You might not remember what gifts you received for your birthday, but you will remember the ice cream shop you always went to. Maybe you'll even continue some traditions with your own children someday.

Sometimes parents have to be involved to get a tradition started, but not always. You and your siblings can do some special little things of your own. And there's no need to save them for big days—traditions can be created for any day of the year. If everyone likes them, you'll have some new ones!

Here are a few ideas to get you started.

Smiles Across the Miles

Start your day with a giggle. Keep a joke book in the family car, and take turns with your siblings reading a joke every day on the way to school.

Funny Farewells

See if you can come up with a silly saying to share with your sibs when you say good-bye. You start with, "See you later, alligator," and your sib says, "After a while, crocodile." Each time you do this, try to add a funny new rhyming line. Some examples: "Bye-bye, little fly." "Gotta go, buffalo." "See you there, baby bear." If you run out of ideas, just use your favorites over and over!

Good Things

At dinner, share one good thing from your day. It could be a big thing, like a top grade on a project, or something small, like seeing cute dogs on a walk. Listen to the things your siblings share, too. This helps remind you to be thankful for all the good things in your life—including one another.

Family Favorites

These traditions are fun for your siblings—and your parents, too!

Family Movie Night

Your family might already have a night of watching movies together. But do you ever watch your *family* movies with your family? Pick a special day, like the first day of summer or Valentine's Day, and watch videos from times when you and your sibs were little or from a favorite vacation.

Breakfast for Dinner

This is a surefire way to cheer everyone up on gloomy days. You and your sibs can help a parent make pancakes, eggs, toast, waffles, smoothies, and whatever else your family likes for breakfast—but do it for dinner! For extra comfort, you can even wear slippers and pj's!

Helping Hands

Lots of families do volunteer work near Thanksgiving, but you can do it any time of year. Talk to your parents and see if this is something your family can do regularly. Volunteering is also a nice way to remember someone you love who lives far away. If you can't be with her, let Grandma know you're helping other people on her birthday.

Musical Memories

Play special songs to make memories all year long. "Happy Birthday to You" isn't the only birthday song in the world—find another one in your family's music collection, or ask an adult to look for one online that you can download. Play that song first thing in the morning on each family member's birthday. Or play a certain song to celebrate going on a vacation, having a snow day, or even the fact that it's Friday!

King or Queen for a Day

Ask a parent to pick up an inexpensive crown or tiara from a costume shop. Then whenever someone in your family does something great, that person gets to wear it for a little while. Maybe you learned to play a piece of music on the piano—wear the tiara! Or your brother mastered a soccer trick—on with the crown! Reminding someone to wear it is almost as much fun as wearing it yourself.

Cute Collection

See if your sister would like to start a collection with you. Pick something sweet, like hearts, or something silly, like gnomes. Then whenever you're out and see something for the collection, buy it for her or take a picture to share with her later.

Any Day's a Holiday

You won't have to wait long for a holiday if you sprinkle a few more of them on the calendar!

National Siblings Day

April 10 is the day to celebrate with your brothers and sisters. Think of something you like to do together, and do it! Or choose one of the ideas from the Boredom Busters chapter starting on page 48.

Half-y Birthday to You

Celebrate your siblings' half birthdays throughout the year. Jot down their real birthdays, and then count six months ahead to find their half birthdays. Have a mini celebration on each of those days. Give a half-sized birthday card, sing a funny half-birthday song, and ask a parent to serve half of a cake for dessert.

Valentines Anytime

Don't wait for Valentine's Day to let your siblings know you love them. Make little valentines for them to find anytime.

Happy Holidaze

Special holidays exist for nearly anything you can imagine. Pickle Day, Puppy Day, and Bike-to-School Day are just a few. Ask a parent to search online for some that might be fun for you and your siblings to celebrate.

Longest Day and Shortest Day

Invite your siblings to mark the summer solstice (longest day of the year) and winter solstice (shortest day of the year) with fun activities. In summer, maybe your parents will let you get up at sunrise and go to bed at sunset. In winter, maybe you can snuggle up and spend an evening reading or playing games with your family—no TV allowed!

Fan Fun

If your family has a favorite team, show your spirit and make a big game day into a holiday. Everyone should wear team colors, hats, or jerseys. You could make a special snack that you have only when your team is playing. Put together a funny victory dance for when the team scores or a little cheer for when it needs some help. Go, team!

Show Your Support

Let your sibs know how much you care—on good days and bad.

Good Days

"We're going to the championships!"

"I have a solo in the concert!"

"I made the team!"

"My art was chosen for the display!"

When something great happens to siblings, it's even greater for them when they can share it with you. You know better than just about anyone how hard your sister worked for it, or how much your brother hoped for it. So your excitement means more, because you really understand.

Also, one of the best things about families is that people get to talk about how happy and proud they are. Out in the world, it might be considered bragging, but in the family, it's OK to shine. When you celebrate your sib's win, you're adding to the happiness in the house, and that feels good for everyone. Any happy occasion for someone in your family is a good excuse for the whole family to celebrate.

So when your sister gets that piano solo, tell her how proud you are of her. If your brother has a big game or performance coming up, ask whether there's anything you can do to help him prepare. If your sib has a part in a show, get tickets and go!

Maybe there's a little part of you that feels jealous of a sister's or a brother's happy news, though. That's normal, especially if you feel like nothing special has happened to you in a while. But try to shake off those feelings by remembering that something good happening to someone else doesn't say anything about *your* accomplishments at all. Maybe your sib's success will even inspire you or show you the way to a success of your own. And if you can be enthusiastic for your sibling now, she will remember it when it's your turn to shine. That day will come for you, too.

Signs of Celebration

★ Make a banner for your sibling with a message of congratulations or encouragement.

★ Put together a playlist of songs from the play that your brother is starring in.

★ Write a card telling your sister how much you think she deserves this and how happy you are for her.

★ Ask a parent to help you frame an award, an announcement, a photo, or a program.

. . . and Bad Days

"I didn't get picked for the play."

"I have to wear this cast for a whole month."

"My best friend isn't talking to me."

"The doctor said I can't ever eat anything with gluten in it."

When something hard or disappointing happens to sisters and brothers, they're bound to feel down, at least for a little while. The good news about bad news is that there are things you can do to help your sib feel better.

The best thing you can do is pretty simple: Just listen. You don't have to know how to solve the problem. Sometimes being able to talk about it helps a person feel better, because she knows someone cares. Sometimes thinking out loud helps a person figure out for himself what he needs to do. And when a problem is big enough to change a person's whole life, talking can help that person get used to the new way things are going to be.

So let your brother talk if he wants to. And tell your sister you're sorry about whatever happened. If you have ideas about what your siblings can do, ask if they want to hear them. But it's OK to just listen to what your sib has to say without saying much yourself.

You can also be an even kinder version of your normal self while your sib is in a slump. Maybe you can offer to play your brother's favorite game with him or let your sister have an extra cookie or an extra turn. You can do small favors or let things slide when you usually wouldn't. If your sibling doesn't seem happier right away, don't be discouraged. Your acts of kindness really do make a difference.

Ask a parent for ideas on how to help, too, especially if it's something big. Maybe the doctor said your sister can't eat certain foods anymore. Or maybe your brother broke his leg and has to wear a cast this summer. You and your parents can come up with ways to help your sibling not feel left out and get used to the situation.

Signs of Support

★ Write a note or draw a picture that lets your sister know how much you care.

★ Ask your brother if he'd like to just hang out with you for a while and talk about what's on his mind.

★ Get a book from the library by your sister's favorite author, or a book with information about her problem.

★ Give your sibling a hug—and repeat often!

Thoughtful Things

No matter the reason, you can let your sibling know you're thinking of her with one of these simple ideas.

Caring Coupons

These are fun to make and even more fun for the other person to use. Make a list of things your sister would probably like you to do for her. Try ideas like "Good for making your bed one time" or "Good for doing one of your chores." Write them on slips of paper, decorated to look like coupons. Tuck them into an envelope, and give them to your sib.

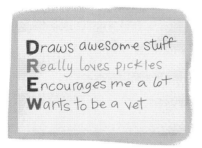

Personal Poem

Write the letters of your brother's name vertically on a piece of paper. Then use each letter to start a line of a poem about him. Try to capture his personality and some of the things you love most about him.

Banner Day

Make signs cheering your brother on to victory! Write encouraging messages on colorful pieces of paper. Place them where he will be happy—or maybe surprised—to see them. Inside a desk drawer, in his backpack, and on the chair where he usually sits for breakfast are all good places.

Happy Book

Put together a cute little book that your sister can flip through whenever she needs a smile. Fold colored paper to make the book. Trim photos of her friends and family to fit on the pages and tape them down, or just fill the pages with pictures of things she likes. (Who wouldn't love a book of adorable baby animals?) Add cheerful captions or slogans.

Good Game

If your brother likes brainteasers, create a game with a message in it just for him. Use graph paper to make a word search—don't forget to jot down all the words he needs to look for! Fill in as many words as you want, and then put random letters in the other squares. Tape your game to a sheet of colored paper, and decorate with markers or stickers. Add a note and give it to your sib.

A Little Luck

If your sister could use a little luck, give her a special token. Find a small plastic figurine or animal, and write a note to go with it explaining that it will bring her luck. Give it to her to tuck into a pocket or backpack. Every time she comes across it, she'll know you're wishing her luck!

Super Siblings

Girls like you share their thoughts on siblings helping siblings.

When I was eight, I broke my ankle. I was too small to use crutches, and it hurt too much to walk. My sister helped me with chores and getting up the stairs. It would have been so much harder without her.
LILY, AGE 10

My brother got a really bad haircut. The stylist had been rough, and it was cut way too short. He was in tears. I gathered a few of my things he loved and gave them to him. He was instantly smiling.
MADDIE, AGE 11

I have really bad stage fright, so when it came to the day of my piano recital, I was really nervous. I thought I couldn't do it. My sister encouraged me and gave me helpful stage hints. I don't think I could have done it without her.
BRIELLE, AGE 11

I was really upset about my parents' divorce, and my big sister cheered me up by buying me ice cream and making time to play with me. She helped me through a difficult time, even when I think she was hurting from the divorce, too.
MAYA, AGE 9

I was sick on Halloween one year, and that meant I couldn't trick-or-treat. When I woke up the day after Halloween, there was a cauldron of candy at my door! My brother had given me a portion of his candy because he knew I was upset!
ELLE, AGE 12

I lost my dance competition, and I was sad. So when my sister heard about it, she made me a ribbon saying "#1 Dancer and Sister."
BECCA, AGE 10

When my sister was going on her first trip away from home—to New York City!— I surprised her by making a "New York fun pack." It was filled with letters, pictures, and a miniature teddy bear. She told me later that it really brought her comfort while away.
JULIE, AGE 11

Someone who used to be my best friend was acting so differently than she used to and was so bossy that I didn't want to be her friend anymore. I was confused, so I talked to my brother. We talked for more than an hour, and I finally knew what to do. That helped me so much, and I'll never forget it!
LILI, AGE 11

I'm an only child, so I don't have any siblings, but I'm very close with my cousins. Recently, I tried out for a dance team and didn't make it. I was pretty bummed, so my cousins came over. They brought a bag of my favorite candy and just hung out with me for the day. They made me feel so much better.
ALLISON, AGE 13

My brother really helped me when I had cancer. He helped me in and out of my bed, he helped me eat and drink when I wasn't feeling well, and he all-around made the experience better for me, even though I didn't think that was possible.
LAUREN, AGE 14

Real Sister Story

OLIVE

AS A MIDDLE CHILD, 12-year-old Olive is both a big sister and a little sister. What's different about her family is that it's bigger than most. Olive is in the middle of six kids!

Her oldest brother is 16, and the baby of the family is 3. What's the best part about having five siblings? "You always have something to do," says Olive. "And there's a variety of options. So if I wanted to play the piano, I might do that with my oldest brother. And if I wanted to read a book, I might talk to my sister who's just older than me about what book to read."

Although they live in the United States now, Olive's family recently moved back after living in a small town in France for more than two years. The siblings relied on one another to get used to their new home—and their new language. "When we moved there, we all knew how to say hello," says Olive, "and that was it!" They attended French school, which was taught in French, of course. To learn the language, they studied together at home. "Whenever one of us learned a new word, we would tell each other what it meant so we could use it at school." Eventually, with one another's help, Olive and her siblings learned to speak French. "We left France with tons of friends and a lot of memories," she says.

So they could document their time in France, Olive and her siblings created videos. "At first it was going to be a talk show," says Olive, "with me being the host and interviewing everybody. But then we decided to make the videos be about our lives and relationships."

Anyone in the family could come up with an idea to film, and the topics included visiting a bakery, gardening, and a trip to a farm. "It was such a fun thing to do with all my siblings," she says. "They were all super energetic and excited about filming." Best of all, the six brothers and sisters have their adventures recorded. "Now we can always remember," says Olive. ♥

BONJOUR

FRANCE

Ma famille

PJ Party Anytime

Celebrate your sisterhood with a sibling slumber party! Any night will do—these ideas don't need much fuss to be fun.

Friends in the House

One of the best things about being a sibling is having someone around for fun any time of the day—or night.

If you think of your sibling as a friend, you will have a lot of opportunities for good times together. Without much planning, you can even have a sib slumber party!

The ideas in this chapter use items you probably have at home already, and you can easily add more ideas if you want to make the party bigger. But sometimes just sleeping in a different spot and making a few snacks is party enough.

Plan a sibling slumber party for a big occasion, like the last day of school or the first night of a stay-at-home vacation. You can also do it as a last-minute way to spice up a dull week. You can even turn it into a regular event—put a few slumber parties on the calendar, and you and your siblings will automatically have something to look forward to. And if you have brothers or sisters who live with you only some of the time, a slumber party can be a fun way to celebrate being together.

Camp In

Pull out some camping gear and have an indoor adventure in your family room!

★ Spread out blankets and fluff pillows.

★ Fill backpacks with everything you need—a good book, a pencil, a sketch pad or journal, lip balm, and your glasses case.

★ Fill water bottles for late-night sipping.

★ Grab flashlights for after-dark reading of your favorite camping stories.

Actually, you don't even need to have a *slumber* party to enjoy this chapter. You can invite a sibling to make one of the snacks anytime, or play one of the games after dinner some evening, or pitch your tents but sleep in your own beds. (Safety tip: Home-made tents are fun to play in, but don't sleep in them.) Good times with your sibling don't have to cost money or take a lot of planning. Just doing things a little bit differently makes them memorable for a long time.

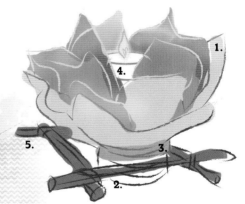

Fake Fire

Add a little glow to the room with this cute campfire craft. **1.** Use scissors to cut two squares of **tissue paper**. Red, yellow, and orange all work well. **2.** Wrap the squares around a small, clear **plastic container**. **3.** Secure with a **rubber band**. **4.** Place a **battery-powered flicker votive** inside the container. (Safety tip: NEVER use a real candle!) **5.** Arrange **sticks** around the bottom. You can almost smell the s'mores!

Family Food

Make yummy snacks and sweet treats from ingredients you might already have.

Mix and Match

Set up a make-a-mix station. Put out small bowls containing whatever tasty tidbits you have. Some great options include **popcorn, cereal** (sweetened or not), **raisins, dried cherries, pretzels, chocolate chips, cheese crackers, mini chocolate candies, nuts,** and **peanut butter sandwich crackers.** Each sibling gets a small bowl and makes his or her own mix.

TIP! Mix just a handful to start, in case you don't like the flavor combinations. Or try one of these combos:

★ Crazy Crunchy: Mix pretzels, popcorn, and cheese crackers.

★ Sweet & Salty: Mix popcorn, chocolate chips, and raisins.

★ Chewy Chippy: Mix raisins and dried fruit with nuts and chocolate chips.

Try each other's treats, and see which ones you like the best!

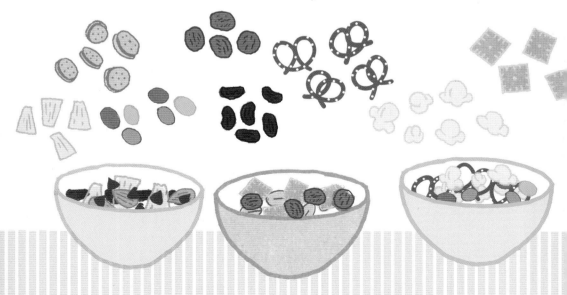

Dip It

Use small bowls of **chocolate and vanilla pudding** as dips for **cookies, fruit,** and other treats. Make up your own combos, or try one of these:

★ S'more: Dip graham crackers and marshmallows into chocolate pudding.

★ Tutti Fruity: Use a fork to dip banana slices and strawberries into vanilla pudding.

★ Can't-Resist Twist: Dip chocolate and vanilla cookies into a swirl of chocolate and vanilla pudding.

Pizza Bites

Make bite-sized pizza rolls! **1.** Place a **tortilla** on a microwave-safe plate. **2.** Spread **pizza sauce** on top. **3.** Sprinkle on some **cheese,** and ask an adult to microwave it just until the cheese melts. Let it cool. **4.** Starting at one edge of the tortilla, roll it up tightly. **5.** Ask an adult to slice it with a butter knife, with the seam side down, and serve.

1.   **2.**

3.

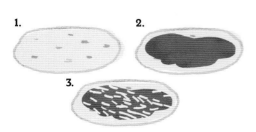

4.   **5.**

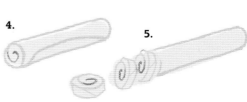

Fun for Two (or More!) to Do

These games will keep you busy until bedtime.

Who's There?

The object of this game is to see how many knock-knock jokes you can make up, all based on this one:

Knock, knock!

Who's there?

The interrupting cow.

The interrup—

(The joke-teller interrupts by saying) **Moooo!**

To start playing, one person tells this joke. Then the next person makes up a similar joke with a different interrupting thing, like this:

Knock, knock!

Who's there?

The interrupting baby.

The interrup—

Waaah! Waaah!

See how silly you can get and how dramatically you can interrupt. Players get one point every time they make someone laugh. (Cracking yourself up doesn't count!) The winner is the one with the most points when you get too tired to make up any more jokes.

Turn It Down!

Nothing on TV? Then make your own show! Turn the TV's volume all the way down. Find a show with people talking. You choose one or two characters to play, and your sib chooses the others. Make up dialogue for your characters, using funny voices and trying to make the words match the person's mouth. If your people get really happy, you should, too. If they get angry or cry, then so do you. You'll be laughing whether your characters are or not!

LOL

Try this silly brainteaser. Think of a new acronym like LOL (laughing out loud). Then use it in a sentence and see if your sib can figure it out. "I'm hungry, because all they had for lunch at school today was meatloaf, and IDLM" (I don't like meatloaf). TI—IF! (Try it—it's fun!)

I Hear with My Little Ear

Try this twist on a favorite game. Look around the room for something that makes a sound. The other person has to try to guess what it is by asking questions that can be answered with a yes or no. The person can also ask what the sound is like: Is it music? Is it repetitive? Is it a nature sound? Is it very quiet? See if you can play this game without asking anything about what the object *looks* like. When your sib guesses correctly, switch roles and play again.

Find Your Space

Being part of a family means there's a special place where you fit—physically *and* emotionally.

You're in It Together

Think about the place that your family calls home sweet home.

Maybe you live in a big house, and you and your siblings all have your own bedrooms with plenty of space for spreading out.

Or maybe there's a lot of togetherness in your family, because your home is smaller or your family is bigger—or both!

Or maybe you're like most sisters, and your situation is somewhere in between.

No matter where you live, being in a family means sharing space. When everyone is getting along, living together can be comfortable, cozy, and fun. There's always someone to talk to, someone to play with, and someone to make you laugh. But sometimes space can feel tight, like everyone is overlapping a bit too much, and that can be hard. Keeping a few tips in mind will help make your home a nicer place for everyone.

Togetherness Tips

1. This one is the simplest of all, but it's pretty important: If you take something out, put it away when you're done with it. If everyone gets into this habit, you won't have to spend as much time picking up or looking for things. And a neater space helps everyone feel more friendly.

2. Be welcoming! If your brother wants to share the table for a project, make room for him. If your sister wants to watch TV with you, scoot over so she can sit down.

3. If you walk into a room or open a closet and see something that needs to be cleaned up or put away, do it if you have time, even if you didn't make the mess. Try not to get hung up on fairness—think of it as a small act of kindness toward your family.

4. Be considerate of what your sibs need, too. Use headphones to listen to music when others need quiet. Keep your own stuff under control in the common areas. Let your little sister and her friends take over the family room once in a while. You'll set a great example for getting along.

5. It's easier to live in a house that's not stuffed with stuff. With a parent's help, go through your things regularly and toss, recycle, sell, or donate items you don't use anymore. Start with your clothes, but also look at your books, toys, knickknacks, sports equipment, and school papers.

6. Notice when you need to get away for a while—maybe before a small annoyance turns into a big fight—and seek a little solitude. A little time alone can make your time together better.

Make Room

Sharing space with a sister or brother can be fun if you each have enough room for your stuff—and yourselves. Whether it's a bedroom, playroom, or study space, these tips will make it easier to know where everything goes.

Hanger Up

If you share a closet, get two different colors of hangers, one for your clothes and one for your sister's. You'll be able to tell at a glance whose shirt is whose.

Instant Messages

Make a spot where you and your sibs can leave notes for each other. Ask an adult to hang a chalkboard or message board, then leave messages—or just doodle decorations!

Neat Nest

A room that looks good is a nicer place to be. Keeping your bed neat goes a long way toward making the whole room look more inviting. Try to get in the habit of making your bed every day. See if you can inspire your sister to do the same.

Night Lights

It can be frustrating if one of you is trying to sleep while the other has the lights on to read. To prevent grumpiness, get a clip-on book light for each of you. That way, the sleepy sister can snooze while the night-owl sister reads away.

File a While

Keeping your important papers safe—and separate—is critical. Get reusable plastic envelopes or expanding file folders in different colors for each of you. You can use them to park papers that are going out and quickly store incoming papers that you need to keep. Go through the files every few days to keep things organized.

Decorating Duo

If possible, find space for each of you to have your own pictures, posters, and decorations so that you can each show your style. You might also enjoy having a shared space that you take

turns decorating. It can be the top of a bookshelf, a small table, or a windowsill. Surprise each other with new displays for holidays, seasons, and events such as back-to-school.

Double Up

Even though it's best not to have too much stuff in your space, some things are so handy that it's worth having one for each of you. You might find it helpful to have your own alarm clock, tape, tissues, pens and pencils, sticky notes—and anything else you use a lot.

Perfectly Private

No matter how much you love being with your siblings, a little time and space for yourself makes it easier for everyone to live together.

Why do you need privacy? A few reasons are pretty obvious . . .

★ You probably don't want the whole family marching through the bathroom while you're in there blow-drying your hair. And you might not enjoy having your little sister barge in while you're getting dressed.

★ When a friend comes to visit, it's fair to want to spend time with just your friend—and without siblings trying to join you.

★ After a busy day of school and activities, you might need to just read, draw, or zone out for a little while. Time by yourself is important, and time without noise is actually soothing for the brain. Everyone needs quiet time to relax.

★ If you have homework to do and your sister keeps asking you questions or your brother has the TV on, it's hard to concentrate. You need some privacy to get your work done.

Think about how much time you need to yourself. If you feel there's not a good balance between time with your family (and friends) and time to yourself, ask your parents for help. Here are a few privacy pointers for you and your parents to talk about.

Knock First

Have a family rule: If a bathroom or bedroom door is closed, everyone knocks. If you need some privacy, you can just close your door. Try making a sign for your doorknob with a privacy message, such as "Recharging Now." Have another rule: If someone knocks on your closed door, the person should wait for you to say, "Come in." If you say, "Just a minute," the knocker will wait (patiently) for the signal that it's OK to enter.

Quiet Time

Set aside a period of quiet time for everyone every day. During this time, the TV, electronic devices, and other sources of sounds should be turned off so that people can read, work, or relax in peace.

Private Place

Find yourself a little space where you can go for peace and privacy. It could be your bedroom, if you don't share it with a sib. Even if you do share, don't give up. Your private place could be a special spot somewhere else in the house, such as a corner in the basement or a large closet. It might also be an outdoor space. Ask your parents to help you make a nook for yourself indoors or out.

Your Place in the Family

Whatever makes you *you,* you fit perfectly in your family.

All siblings are alike in some ways and different in other ways. Some differences just happen, and we can't change them—you might be the oldest child or the only girl in your family, for example. And you were born with your own set of physical features that are different from your siblings'.

You and your sibs also have different likes and dislikes. You're good at different things. And you have different opinions. All these differences help make life interesting for everyone in the family.

You have many similarities, too. You probably live in the same home and share the same family—pets and all. You might go to the same school. You like many of the same foods and want to do some of the same activities. You share jokes and traditions, and you love many of the same stories. The ways you're alike help you feel close to one another.

Your one-of-a-kind combo of differences and similarities is what makes you who you are. It's what defines your special spot in your family.

What Makes You YOU?

How do you want your family to see you?

★ Make a list of words that you think describe you. They can be facts, such as "middle sister" and "tall."

★ Add words like "cheerful," "strong," and "musical"—all the ways you see yourself.

★ Last, add things you're interested in, and things you like to do, such as "love animals" and "soccer."

Look over your list. You should see a pretty clear picture of all the things you enjoy and all your strengths. Does your family know about everything on your list?

Although most kids have a long list, a family might focus on one thing and maybe even call a kid "the sporty one" or "the math expert." Being known for just one thing can be frustrating, because you might feel you always have to be that way—and can't ever be anything else. But what if you don't want to be known for that thing? Or what if you want to dance out you're not "the dancer" in your family? Or maybe you've changed a bit, but your family still thinks of you as how you were before.

Sometimes the people who are closest to you have the hardest time noticing when you've changed, especially when the change is slow. It's like growing taller—when someone hasn't seen you for a long time, it's easy to see how much bigger you've gotten. But to your family, you're pretty much the same size every day. The same goes for the girl you are growing up to be. You might be leaving behind old hobbies and getting new interests, and maybe your family hasn't noticed.

Celebrating Your Place

Here are a few ways—some big and some small—to help your family see who you've become, unique from your siblings.

★ If you're known by one thing you're really good at, let yourself feel happy about it, but at the same time let your family know you're more than that one thing. You can say, "I love to dance. That's part of who I am—but only a part!"

★ Is your family calling you by a nickname you've had since you were little? If you don't like it, ask them to start calling you by your real name, or suggest a new nickname.

★ If your bedroom has been decorated the same way for years and you've outgrown it, talk to a parent about redoing it.

★ Maybe it's time to give up a hobby you don't like anymore and start taking lessons in something you're more excited about.

★ Find a way to celebrate your uniqueness. If that means doing something completely different from your sibs, that's great. But if you really want to try something that already seems to "belong" to your brother or sister, that's OK, too—just do it your own special way.

BAKING

Real Sister Story

AINYR

NINE-YEAR-OLD AINYR (pronounced *eye-NAR*) has a brother who is the same age that she is. But they're not twins!

Ainyr and Erlan *(er-LAHN)* were both born in the Asian country Kazakhstan *(KAH-zahk-stahn)* during the same month of the same year—two weeks apart. They were born in two different families, and they were adopted by the same family in the United States when they were less than a year old. For as long as they can remember, they have been brother and sister. "He's just a little older," says Ainyr.

Ainyr gets asked whether she's a twin all the time, but she doesn't often get asked about adoption. Being adopted is "very cool," she says. "You get to go with a family that will be yours forever. And I really like my family!"

Maybe because she was born in another country, Ainyr likes to travel. "I like the beach at Cape Cod, and I rock-climb," she says.

Every summer, she and Erlan go to a camp away from home, in the town where their grandmother lives. The first day feels a little scary, but they help each other. "I feel more comfortable when my brother's there, and he feels better, too."

For Ainyr, having a brother the same age means liking a lot of the same activities, games, and movies. "We have fun doing things together and also when we have friends over. It's cool being Erlan's sister."

Ainyr (which means "moonbeam") and Erlan ("great warrior") both have the Kazakh names they were born with. One day Ainyr would like to visit Kazakhstan. "It's beautiful," she says, "and it has snow leopards." She and Erlan go to Kazakh cultural events, and their parents have Kazakh art in their home and books about the country of their birth so that they can know about the heritage they share. "The best part about having Erlan as a brother is we understand each other." ♥

CAPE COD

Boredom Busters

Sometimes the secret to feeling closer to your sisters and brothers is just having more fun together, more often. These ideas make it easy to do that. And chances are, you already have everything you need.

Cool 'n' Creative

Back Each Other Up

Sit back-to-back with your brother. He should have paper, markers, and a surface to draw on. You name something, and he draws it. Then you name something else for him to include in his scene. You can be silly or serious, but be as specific as you can. When you're done, look at his drawing. Then it's your turn to draw the things he names.

Cute Collages

Get some old magazines and catalogs, scissors, paper, markers, and glue sticks. Make a collage with pictures and words you know your sibling will love, while your sib does the same for you. Include a few surprises, too. Hang the finished collages in your rooms.

Crazy Coloring

Make a fancy design for your sister to color while she makes one for you. Use a thin black marker to draw loopy scribbles on a piece of paper, filling the whole page. Draw so that there are lots of small spaces for her to fill in. Trade designs, then color in the loops and spaces with crayons or colored pencils, making sure the marker lines don't smear.

A Long Line

Make an arty portrait of your brother. Ask him to sit across from you, and then start drawing. The trick is to draw him in one long line without lifting your marker from the paper. It helps to keep looking at him and not at the paper while you draw. After you're finished, ask him to draw you.

Hair Flair

Do a cute 'do on your sister. Gather all the hair clips you can find. Brush your sister's hair. Starting near the part in her hair, snap in a line of hair clips. Add more lines of clips until you run out of hair—or clips!

It's Supersister!

Make a comic strip about you and your sibling. Maybe your sibling writes the words and you draw the scenes, or maybe you work together on both parts. Create the characters, come up with a short story featuring them, and put it all on paper.

Upside-Down Drawing

This project will get you to see familiar faces in a new way. Find a nice photo of you and a sibling in which both of your faces are pretty big. Turn the photo upside down and draw it. Then let your sibling try. When you're both done, turn your drawings and the photo right side up and compare.

Colorful Closet

Ask a parent and a brother or sister to help you arrange the clothes in your closet by color. When you finish, do the same with your sibling's closet.

Remake a Movie

Try to re-create a short scene from your favorite movie with your sibs. Memorize the lines and the gestures. Practice, practice, practice. Then when you're ready, perform it for your parents or friends!

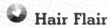

Around the House

Puzzle Place

Find a puzzle you'd like to put together. Set up a puzzle table or corner, and start working on it. Your siblings will probably wander over and join you, because that's what usually happens when someone starts a puzzle!

You Got Games

Make a list of your favorite board games, and then challenge your sister to play all of them. See how long it takes to get through the list. One day? A whole week?

Sibling Switcheroo

Switch places with a sibling for one day (or one hour). Swap pj's or clothes if you have some that fit each other. Stretch out in each other's beds, and start reading whatever book the other is reading. Listen to each other's favorite songs. See the world from your sib's point of view for just a little while.

Ask Your Mom or Dad

Sit down with your brother, and come up with a list of interesting or funny questions to ask your parents, uncle, grandma, or anyone else in your family. It might be fun to do this during dinner or on a long trip. Try these questions, and add a few of your own:

★ What was the first car you remember riding in?
★ What was something you liked to do as a kid that we can't do because it isn't around anymore?
★ How was school different when you were a kid?
★ What were some fashions that were cool when you were younger?
★ Was there ever a collecting craze or fad that you did as a kid?
★ Do you think we would have been friends if we'd known you when you were our age?
★ What are some funny things you did with *your* siblings?

 ## Coin Collecting

If you have a coin jar in your house, use it for fun. Pour out some coins, and sort through them with your sister. Make a list of coins you're looking for, and see if you can find them all. Try these, or come up with your own!

★ Coins from the year you were born
★ State quarters from the state you live in, where your grandpa lives, or . . .
★ The shiniest penny, nickel, dime, and quarter in the jar
★ The oldest penny, nickel, dime, and quarter in the jar

Wash your hands when you're done!

 ## Exclusive Interview

Pretend you've jumped twenty years into the future. Your brother pretends to be a star at whatever he wants to be when he grows up, and you pretend to be a reporter for a cool magazine. Interview your brother and ask him all about his life. Then change places, and he interviews you.

 ## Sister Spa

Pamper yourselves on a weekend day after you've both taken showers. Wear your robes, wrap your hair in towels, and ask a parent to paint your toenails. For the full experience, put on soft music. Put scented lotion on your hands for a bit of aromatherapy. Aaahhh!

Food Fun

 ## Sweet Treat

 Think of someone you and your siblings know who could use a treat. Maybe it's a new neighbor, a family friend who just had a baby, or the driver of your school bus. Ask a parent to help you and your sibs make a batch of your best brownies or bars for that person. While the treats are cooling, make a card to go with the treats. Include a list of the ingredients, just in case the person has food restrictions. Then go together and deliver the goodies with a smile.

 ## Cute Cupcakes

Make a bite with your bro and something sweet with your sis. Ask an adult to help you decorate frosted cupcakes to look like everyone in your family, one for each. Use candies, cereal, and raisins to make hair, eyes, and other features. See if people can guess who is who!

Holiday Favorites

Think of some recipes you like to make for the holidays. Ask an adult to help you and your siblings mix up a batch of your favorite cookies or other treats at a different time of year. One bite will make you feel like the holidays are right around the corner!

Ice Cream Shop

Imagine an ice cream shop that you and your sister could run. What would you call it? See if each of you can come up with new flavors for your shop. For example, maybe strawberry ice cream with chocolate chips could be called Ladybug. Or invent a new sundae—multicolored sherbet with marshmallow sauce and sprinkles could be the Rainbow in a Cloud sundae. Then take a break and have some ice cream for real!

Sister Café

Treat your siblings to a snack at a restaurant that you run yourself. Check with a parent about what snacks you can serve, and create a menu. Choose snacks that don't need to be cooked. Set the table as prettily as you can. A flower in a vase is a nice touch, too. Invite your guests to sit down and order off the menu. Don't forget to keep water glasses filled. If your service is good, maybe you'll get a tip at the end.

Dinner Planner

What's for dinner? It's up to you! With your sister, go through some of your family's cookbooks and food magazines and mark dishes that look tasty. A parent can help you pick a few to try for a special meal, and then you can help your parent prepare them. You may find some new family favorites!

Apples to Zucchini

The next time you and your sibs are at the grocery store, ask a parent if each of you can pick out one new item to try. It can be a type of fruit, vegetable, cheese, bread, or whatever seems interesting. Later, ask everyone in the family to try the new food and see what they think.

Great Outdoors

 ## Good Goal

Choose a goal related to something active that you and your brother and a parent can accomplish together. Try walking, running, or biking a certain number of miles together over a set period of time. Keep track of your progress, and encourage each other. Then reward yourselves when you reach your goal!

 ## Chalk It Up

If the weather is nice, grab a sister and some sidewalk chalk and get busy. Draw a long city scene together, adding buildings, trees, cars, and people. Or create a scene with lots of silly creatures. Safety tip: Ask an adult to help you pick a safe place to draw, such as a sidewalk, that's away from where cars can drive.

 ## Hoop Hoopla

Have some fun with toy hoops! If you can't twirl a hoop around your waist very well, practice and see if you can improve. How long can you keep a hoop going? Swivel with your siblings and see who can go the longest.

 ## Park Rangers

You probably know all the parks near where you live, but does your town have others that you seldom visit—or have never visited? Look at a map and find out! Pick a park you haven't seen recently, and ask a parent to take you and your siblings to check it out. Use a notebook to jot down the park's features—playground equipment, a ball field, a pond, hiking trails, a wilderness area—and give it an overall rating. Keep the notebook and add to it with each new park you visit.

 ## Leaf Pile

With a parent and your siblings, collect one leaf from every tree in your yard and one of every flower. (Safety tip: Stay clear of weeds—some can injure you.) When you're done, see if you can find the names of all the trees and flowers you sampled.

Treasure Hunt

Ask a parent to help you set up a scavenger hunt for your brother in your backyard. First, hide a treasure such as a small toy. Then work backward to make the clues. For example, if you hide the treasure under a bush, go to a tree and leave a note there directing your sib to the bush. Then go to the shed and leave a note pointing your brother to the tree. Write the clues on bright paper to make them easier to find. When you've left a few notes, give your sib the first clue and get going!

Still Together

Grab a beach towel, and head out for some quiet fun with your sister. In the daytime, sit still and see what birds fly by, or lie on your bellies and look for bugs and critters on the ground. Or ask a parent to take you out on a clear night to look for shooting stars, planets, and constellations.

Inside Out

Sometimes it's cool to do something outside that you usually do inside. On the next nice day, invite your siblings to join you outdoors for one of these activities: eating breakfast, reading a book, listening to music, watching a movie, drawing, knitting, or dancing.

Merry Music

 ## Do a Duo

If you and your brother play different instruments, see if you can both learn the same song and play it together, just for fun. If you both play the same instrument, or if one of you doesn't play, one of you can play and the other can sing.

 ## Music Reporters

Chances are, you haven't heard all the music in your family's collection. Ask a parent to pick out some songs or bands for you and your siblings to listen to. Then pretend to be music reporters. Rate the music on originality, catchiness, how easy it would be to dance to, and any other categories you like. Compare your ratings, and see if you find a new family favorite.

 ## Get in the Routine

Be a junior choreographer! Pick out a great dance song, and invite your sister to invent a dance routine with you. Each of you gets to contribute moves and ideas. Keep practicing until you learn the whole thing. Once you know the routine well, you can do it any time the song comes on.

 ## Sing Along

Have a lip-sync party with your family! Everyone dances or plays air instruments like guitar, drums, piano, or trumpet while you take turns lip-syncing to your favorite songs. Ham it up and have a ball!

Accordion Beat Composer

If you and your siblings are into music, you'll like this game. Someone starts by naming anything musical that starts with the letter A. It could be an instrument, a song, a singer, a term, or anything else related to music. The next player names something musical that starts with B. Keep taking turns, and go through the whole alphabet. To add to the challenge, put on some music in the background while you play!

Play Together

Here's another way to play with your sibs: Make some rhythm instruments. See what you have that will make an interesting sound by shaking or tapping it. Look around your house for inspiration. Then put on a song with a good beat and try to play along.

Big Band

Imagine you and your sisters and brothers are in a mega-popular band. What's your band called? What kind of music do you play? Who plays which instrument? What does your logo look like? Talk about it with your sibs and see what you can dream up. You can even try writing and playing a song together for real!

Easy As One, Two, Three

Put on some music, and invent a new dance with your siblings. The first person makes up a simple dance move, such as a step to the right. Then everyone does it. The second person does the first move and adds a new move. So she takes a step to the right and adds a clap, and then everyone does it. The next player does those two moves and adds a new move, and all the players follow. Go around until everyone has added a move, and then repeat the whole sequence until the song ends.

Family Vacations

You'll always remember trips with your family. These ideas will help you and your siblings make wonderful memories together!

Going Places

Whether your family camps, visits theme parks, goes on cruises, takes road trips, or flies to new adventures, your vacations can be some of the best times you spend together.

A family vacation doesn't have to be fancy to be one of the most memorable times of your life. And you and your siblings are all in it together.

Because you're exploring new places and having adventures together, family vacations can make you feel really close to your siblings. You'll bounce ideas off each other. You'll laugh about funny stuff and get excited about new sights and experiences. Your sisters and brothers are your travel buddies, seeing the world with you, and you'll talk about what you saw and what you did long after the vacation is over—maybe for the rest of your lives!

Of course, vacations can also have stressful moments. Hours spent in a car or on a plane can make you crabby. Long days and late bedtimes can make you overtired. Tons of excitement and too much junk food can make you feel a little out of control. Here are some tips to keep you and your sibs feeling good and ready to go:

★ Spend a little of each day just relaxing and having some quiet time.

★ Take a short walk with a parent.

★ Read a book instead of flipping on the TV.

★ Eat when meals are served so you aren't relying on snacks or unhealthy food to get through the day.

★ Do your best to get a good night's sleep.

Fair Is Fair

Whether it's time to pick the day's activities, the restaurant for lunch, or who gets to sleep in which bed, these tips will help make sure everyone gets a chance to choose.

Bug–Leaf–Chicken

This is a fun twist on the game Rock–Paper–Scissors. The hand shapes are the same, but

 is a bug,

 is a leaf, and

 is a chicken.

To play, each person makes a fist and waves it sideways as you chant "bug, leaf, chicken!" On "chicken," all players make one of the shapes with their hand. Here's how to win:

★ A chicken can eat a bug.

★ A bug can eat a leaf.

★ A leaf can cover the chicken's eyes so that it can't see.

Try this a couple of times. The person who wins two out of three gets to choose something.

Roll It

A pair of dice can be used a bunch of ways to see who gets to pick something. Try one of these games:

Birth order. Figure out who is the oldest (1), the next oldest (2), and so on until everyone has a number. Roll one die. The person whose number comes up gets to choose. If no one's number comes up, roll again until someone's does.

Write a list of your first names in alphabetical order. The first person's name is 1, the next is 2, and so on until everyone has a number. Roll one die. The person whose number comes up gets to choose. Next time, try putting the names in reverse alphabetical order.

If everyone who wants to choose is between 2 and 12 years old, just roll both dice until they add up to one of the players' ages. That person gets to pick!

Travel Tips

Girls like you share their best boredom busters for traveling in a car or plane.

I have long heart-to-hearts with my sister. Sometimes we're so busy with friends and school activities that we don't get to spend a lot of time together. It's fun just sitting and talking with her.
SOPHIA, AGE 11

I make up songs with my brother. We sing about things we pass, like a giant snowman or a trio of jets. It's so much fun!
ANNA, AGE 12

My favorite boredom buster is called the Horse Game. When you're riding in a car and see horses, you yell, "My horses!" If you are the first one to say it, you get 1 point for each horse and 11 points for a white horse.
KIRSTIN, AGE 11

I usually tell stories to my younger sisters. They love it! It makes me use my imagination and takes my mind off the question "How much longer?"
LILY, AGE 13

We usually play a pretend cooking game. First, you agree on five ingredients that you have to use in your dish, and then, using those five ingredients, you make up a recipe for a meal. My dad decides which sounds best, and he names the champion!
HANNAH, AGE 12

Before long car rides, my brother and I make our own road bingo game. It has things to find like a red car, a barn, or a spotted cow. Whoever checks off a row of them wins.
OLIVIA, AGE 12

My brother and I like to listen to audiobooks on long rides. We love listening to a good, exciting story while gazing out the window. It seems to make the trip go faster! We also like to play a game called Banana. When we see a yellow car, we say, "Banana!" Whoever sees the most yellow cars wins!
AIDAN, AGE 11

When I'm bored in the car, we play this game where someone says three words that are as silly as they can be, and then we use them in a story. It's really fun!
MAEGAN, AGE 11

My family is very musical, so on long car rides we all sing songs from movies and old TV shows together. We have a good time singing and laughing.
MIA, AGE 12

Photo Fun

Wherever you go, you're sure to snap pictures of your trip. Try these ideas for special shots with your sibs.

Beach Buds

With your parents and siblings, use sticks to write your names and the year in the sand. Then sit or stand by your names while someone takes your picture. Safety tip: Never go near the water without an adult.

Get Ahead

Line up with your family behind a short wall so that only your heads and shoulders show along the edge. Take a shot with everyone wearing hats or making funny faces.

Jump Shots

Jump excitedly in the air with your brother in front of a landmark or beautiful scene while someone snaps your picture.

Frame It

Stand across from your sister, arms open sideways to make it look like you are framing a monument with your arms.

Prop It Up

Bring a small doll or stuffed animal from home that you can photograph on all your adventures. Take turns posing with it.

ART You Glad We're on Vacation?

In this picture, pose with your sister exactly like a sculpture in a park. Be super silly!

Make Memories

When you get home, make these projects with your sibling to squeeze a little more fun out of your vacation.

Vacation in a Box

Ask your family to jot down on slips of paper some favorite memories of the trip. Put the paper slips into a box. Add small souvenirs that you and your sibs collected, such as seashells, brochures, and rocks. Close the box and label it with the name of your vacation spot and the year. Whenever you want to relive the trip, just open the box!

Bind a Book

A scrapbook is another great way to remember a trip. Work with your sibs on each page, and include photos, postcards, drawings, ticket stubs, and other fun, flat mementos. Or have each person do a page or two, and collect them all in one book.

Frame Your Family

Pick a favorite vacation photo of you with your siblings. Get a frame with a wide mat included that will fit the photo. Ask an adult to remove the mat from the frame. Have everyone in the photo sign his or her name on the mat near the opening for the photo. Ask a parent to frame it—you will treasure it for years to come!

Real Sister Story

BELLA

LOTS OF GIRLS have big sisters. But Bella's two sisters are MUCH bigger—in fact, they are adults! Ariel, who is 24, is a college student, and Aubre is 30 years old and an author.

Bella and her sisters were born in three different states in three different decades. When Bella was born, Aubre was home from college and was there to hold her newborn sister. Ariel was in middle school then, and she left for college when Bella was 7. Bella is 11 now, so she's been the only girl living at home for a few years.

Bella loves visits with her big sisters. They can drive, so they take her places when they get together. "They always try to include me," she says. "They're really sweet."

Another fun fact about Bella is that because Aubre is married, Bella has a brother-in-law. Bella got to be a junior bridesmaid in the wedding, and she loved taking part in all the preparations with her big sisters. "It was especially fun getting our hair done," she says.

Even though they are separated by many miles, Bella stays close with her sisters. They started a long-distance book club together, and they use social media to keep in touch, sending pictures and text messages to one another. "Also, they've helped me with multiple problems," Bella says. If she's having trouble, she likes getting advice from her older sisters. "They might have been through it before!"

Bella looks forward to the holidays, when she usually gets to see both Aubre and Ariel. "That's when everyone tries to get together in our family," she says. Bella's birthday is a few days after Christmas, so her sisters are often there to celebrate with her.

The best part of having older sisters? Bella says, "They are role models for me." ♥

BOOK CLUB

love

New Additions

Finding out that you will be getting a new brother or sister is exciting news. You might also feel a little worried, wondering what changes are coming your way. These ideas will help you welcome and enjoy your new family member.

Big News

"Our new baby will be born in May!"

"We're adopting a little boy."

"You'll be a big sister!"

"When we get married, Maddie will become your stepsister."

Your parents told you something BIG—you're going to have a new sibling! How did you feel when you heard the news? Excited? Happy? Maybe a little nervous? Maybe a *lot* nervous? However you felt is OK, because there's no one right way to feel about getting a sibling. A new family member always means some changes, and it can be hard to imagine what life will be like after he or she comes.

What will change? If a new baby is coming, your parents will need to spend time just taking care of him, because of course a baby can't take care of himself. If an older child is joining your family, it will take time for her to adjust, and she'll need help and kindness from everyone. If you're getting a new stepsibling because a parent is getting married, your family is growing in more ways than one, and there will be lots of new routines to try out. Your parents may be extra busy for a while, but they are still there for you, especially if you're feeling down or have a problem.

Some days you may be happily daydreaming about the fun you'll have with your new sib, and some days you may be worried without even really knowing why. That's OK. Talking to your parents about what will change will help you be prepared. Ask questions. Share your excitement and your worries. And remember that even though your family is growing, your special place in it will never change, and your parents love you as much as ever.

Look for ways to be part of the preparations for your new sibling. Help your parents find a fun way to announce the big news to your family and friends. Whether you'll be living with a new baby or an older child, learn as much as you can about your new sister or brother. Depending on your situation, that might mean taking a babysitting class or finding out more about the country where your sib will be coming from. Ask your parents for ideas on ways to get involved, too. No matter what you like to do, there's sure to be a way you can use your talents to get ready.

Look for ways to stay connected to your parents. Grab a quick hug. Pitch in with a chore and take advantage of the chance to talk. And ask to schedule something you love to do together, like going to the library, taking a bike ride, or watching a favorite show.

Welcome Home

No matter how your new sibling will be joining the family, these ideas will show what a super sister you are.

Nice Name

Create pretty artwork of your new sister's name for her room. Cut a piece of colored paper the same size as a small frame. Write her name on the paper, and add colorful doodles and designs. Ask an adult to put your creation in the frame.

Parent's Helper

Ask your parents how you can help them get ready for the big day. Can you go with them to shop for new clothes or supplies for your new brother? Clean out a closet to free up storage space? Learn how to do something for yourself to give them a little more time? Preparing ahead of time will give you all more time for fun after your sib arrives.

Story Time

For a new younger sister, get a copy of a book you loved when you were little. You can buy a new copy, or pass along your old one if you can bear to part with it. Write something sweet inside the front cover. Then read the book to your sib as often as she asks for it!

Say Cheese!

If you have a camera, use it to take lots of pictures of your new brother. You'll have a unique perspective that your parents won't have in the pictures they take. Plus, you'll be able to get your parents in some of the photos, too, which you will all like seeing in the years to come.

From the Heart

Write a letter to your new sister. Share some of the thoughts and wishes you had before she arrived, and tell the story of what it was like to meet her for the first time. Include some dreams you have for the future and fun things you'd like to do together when you are both older. Ask a parent to tuck it away for safekeeping, perhaps in her baby book.

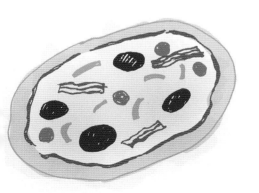

Something Old, Something New

Invite new stepsiblings to join your fun family traditions, like Pizza Fridays. Be willing to try some of their family traditions, too—maybe they have Pancake Saturdays. And work together to come up with new traditions, like Nature Walk Sundays. Or turn to the Everyday Magic chapter starting on page 8 for more ideas on starting traditions!

Sweet Sisters

Girls share their thoughts about new siblings.

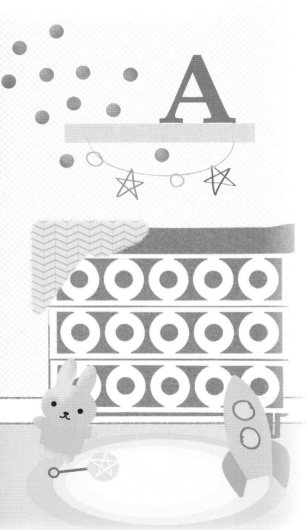

When I got a three-year-old stepsister, I gave her chocolate cupcakes. I put them in a tin and she loved them! Now she's five, and we still get along really well.
ANASTASIA, AGE 10

When my little brother was born, he was the cutest thing. Although I was small, I tried to help in every way, whether it was helping to feed him or trying to calm him down when he was in one of his moods. I loved him so much and still do.
RACHEL, AGE 13

I absolutely love home decorating, so when I heard I was going to have a baby sister, I got moving! I designed her room, and then my dad and I put it together in the room that used to be my playroom. My sister is now one and a half years old, and she loves her bedroom.
ELAINE, AGE 12

My sister and I doted on my youngest brother when he was born. We helped my mom take care of him in all sorts of different ways, from singing him lullabies to reading him books. We think he's the most precious thing in the world!
CHLOE, AGE 14

I couldn't wait to welcome my little sister home. I have a big sister, and I have always looked up to her and counted on her for advice. I was eager to have a little sister I could offer advice to. Now, each year on my birthday, I write a short letter of advice for my little sister that she can open on her corresponding birthday. For example, my sister is turning eight this year, and she will open the letter I sealed for her on my eighth birthday.
TRINA, AGE 11

My mom had a baby girl yesterday! I bought a cake and even made a painting of a rose for her. I have one older sister and now I have a younger sister, too, so I am happy!
CAYLYNN, AGE 12

I have one birth brother and two sisters who were adopted from Africa. We adopted my first sister when I was six. I was really excited, and it was the coolest thing ever to have a little sister from another part of the world! It took a lot of paperwork, and the week that my dad left to bring her home was hard, but my sister was definitely worth the wait. A few years later, we decided it was time to adopt again. This time, though, I didn't have to just wait. I got to go to Africa! It was the experience of a lifetime. When I grow up, I want to go back and work with people there. My favorite part of the trip was meeting my new sister. Now my family is a lot bigger, and we all love each other very much.
EVELEA, AGE 13

Rough Stuff

One of the hardest—but most normal!—things about being a sister is sibling squabbles. Whether they happen every day or just once in a while, this advice should help smooth out the bumps.

Fair Fights

If you and your siblings are fighting, it means you're trying to figure out how to work out a problem.

Fights are no fun. But learning how to get through problems with siblings is great practice for life—even grown-ups have disagreements! Arguments can help you figure out how to deal with differences and how to handle feeling upset without making the problem worse.

The way you fight can help you solve the problem—or it can keep you feeling bad or fighting about it. Here are a few Fair Fight rules to start practicing now. The more you follow them, the better you will get at them, and the faster your fights will end.

1. Stick to the subject. NO FAIR bringing up other problems or fights you've had in the past.

2. Talk about how the problem makes you feel right now. NO FAIR saying your sibling *always* does something or *never* does something. That's probably not true, and it's definitely not helpful.

3. Speak calmly. NO FAIR yelling.

4. Listen to what your sibling has to say. NO FAIR interrupting.

5. Be ready to forgive when the fight is done. NO FAIR staying mad if your sib has made a real effort to solve the problem or apologize, or if you don't get your way.

Important!

Even if you're really mad, try to stay calm, and remember that once you say something mean, you can't *unsay* it. A fight will eventually end, but hurt feelings can last a long time. Keep that from happening: Take deep breaths. Count to 10. Say you'll be right back, and leave the room until you can calm down. And try to find the words that will help you end the fight instead of keeping it going.

Things to say to help end a fight:

Maybe there's an easy way we can work this out. What do you think?

I understand why you're mad. Let's talk about it when we're both calm.

I don't want to be mad, but I need to tell you how I feel and what I would like to happen next time. Can we talk?

Can we just sit down together and talk about it? I'll listen while you tell me your side.

How about if you use it for 10 minutes, and then it's my turn?

Saying "Sorry"

Being able to apologize the right way will help you and your siblings stay close.

Maybe it'll be for something small, like spilling your milk on him at dinner. Maybe it'll be for something big, like saying something that you knew would hurt her feelings. Apologizing is a sign of strength and maturity, and it will help you and your siblings be good friends. Here's how to do it:

You have to actually be sorry.

Saying you're sorry before you're ready usually doesn't help bring a fight to an end. If you need to say it but you're not feeling it yet, it's better to cool off a little and wait to apologize until you mean it.

Instead of this:
"Well, SORRY!"

Or this:
"Don't be so sensitive. I was just joking."

Say this:
"I'm sorry. I was trying to be funny, but it came out wrong. I didn't mean to hurt you."

Take responsibility.

If something was your fault, don't be afraid to admit it. Making excuses, changing the subject, or blaming the person you're apologizing to only makes things worse.

Instead of this:
"I'm sorry I borrowed your shirt without asking you, but you always take my stuff when I'm not here."

Say this:
"I'm sorry I borrowed your shirt without asking. I should have asked first."

Look the person in the eye when you say it.

It may feel awkward, but try not to look down at your feet or mumble. Say what you need to say in a calm voice. Keep it simple.

Instead of this:
"mumble mumble sorry mumble"

Say this:
"I'm sorry."

When you mean it—really mean it—people can tell. And that's when the bad feelings start to float away.

Accept an apology.

When a sibling says, "I'm sorry" to you, it may be tempting to give one of these replies:

". . ." No reply just leaves the apologizer hanging there.

"That's OK." If what he did was not OK, don't say it was, even if you're done fighting about it.

"Whatever." If you're still mad, you need to talk it out with your sib.

"Yeah, that was really bad!" If your sister has sincerely apologized, it's OK to say how you felt, but it's not fair to make her keep repeating that she's sorry.

If your sib is sorry and you're ready to move on, all you have to say is, "Thank you for saying you're sorry" or "Apology accepted."

Moving On

When you're upset, any problem can feel big. But some problems are less serious than others.

Sometimes the thing you're fighting about seems a little silly after it's over. Maybe it's about who has the remote control or who gets to sit by the window. Maybe it's who ate the last cupcake or whose turn it is to choose the movie. It may be something that you've argued about before.

Think about the kinds of things that start you and your siblings arguing. There are probably a few situations that come up again and again. For the ones that really bother you or seem to spark a lot of spats, pick a time when things are calm and ask a parent to help you talk this through or come up with solutions.

★ Can your family set up a system for taking turns?
★ What are the rules about using an item that belongs to the whole family?
★ What if there's only one of something and two people want it?

If you and your sibs can find ways to make things work better, you'll spend less time being upset or annoyed—and more time having fun and getting things done together.

Another way to handle a small problem is to pause before you jump into battle. Ask yourself if there's a better way to deal with the situation than arguing.

★ Do you already have a solution planned for this problem?
★ Is it actually your sister's turn?
★ Can you say what you need to say with a calm voice instead of an angry one?

Or maybe this time you can decide to just take a deep breath and let it go. You could let your sister be the one to pick the cereal at the store, even if she picked it last week, too. You could let your brother have the first turn when you play a game, even if it seems he always gets to go first.

Your feelings count, and fairness matters. But it might help to remember that fair is not the same thing as equal. Everyone doesn't always get the exact same thing, for example, and one person will have to go first. Things usually even out over time, though. And in the end, being generous might actually feel better than winning a fight.

Real
Sister Story

CHLOE & GRACIE

IN A LOT OF WAYS, Chloe and Gracie are like many other sisters. They love some of the same music, and they play board games, go swimming, and play with their three dogs together. And like many big sisters, Chloe, age 12, looks out for 9-year-old Gracie. "When I was little, she used to walk me to the park so I wouldn't get hurt," says Gracie.

But one day, Chloe *really* looked out for Gracie—she actually saved Gracie's life. Gracie wasn't feeling well that morning and decided a bath might help her feel better. Because of the hot water and her fever, Gracie's brain had a seizure, which caused her to lose consciousness.

When her mom yelled for help, Chloe came running. She performed cardiopulmonary re-suscitation (or CPR) while the girls' dad called for an ambulance. Soon, thanks to Chloe's quick action, Gracie was breathing again.

Gracie was in the hospital for several days, and during that time Chloe didn't want to leave her side. After her little sister came home, Chloe received two awards for her actions. The first one was given by Gracie's doctor. The second was given by the chief of the fire department for being the youngest person in their state to save a life. How did Chloe know how to do CPR? "I learned it that year in my school," she explains.

Gracie is healthy now, and these days the sisters are back to doing what sisters do. Gracie likes dance video games and playing with her friends, and she still loves bubble baths. Chloe tried scuba diving and wants to get certified soon. And she is glad that she knows how to do CPR. "It was good to learn it," she says, and she thinks other people should learn it, too. And like many little sisters, Gracie looks up to her big sister. "I feel so grateful to have Chloe as a sister!" ♥

lifesaver

SCUBA

Write to Us!

Send your sister ideas and true stories to

The Sister Book Editor

American Girl

8400 Fairway Place

Middleton, WI 53562

All comments and suggestions received by American Girl may be used without compensation or acknowledgment. We're sorry—we're unable to return photos.